This journal belongs to

_____

...BECAUSE I AM AWESOME!

...BECAUSE I AM AWESOME!

Interactive JOURNAL

DIANE A. THOMPSON, MD

...BECAUSE I AM AWESOME! JOURNAL
Published by Purposely Created Publishing Group™
Copyright © 2020 Diane A. Thompson

All rights reserved.

No part of this book may be reproduced, distributed or transmitted in any form by any means, graphic, electronic, or mechanical, including photocopy, recording, taping, or by any information storage or retrieval system, without permission in writing from the publisher, except in the case of reprints in the context of reviews, quotes, or references.

Printed in the United States of America

ISBN: 978-1-64484-241-6

Special discounts are available on bulk quantity purchases by book clubs, associations and special interest groups.
For details email: sales@publishyourgift.com or call (888) 949-6228.
For information log on to: www.PublishYourGift.com

I.

I am

admirable

because I'm deserving of
and command respect.

LIST 3 THINGS THAT MAKE YOU ADMIRABLE.

1. _____

_____

_____

_____

_____

2. _____

_____

_____

_____

_____

3. _____

_____

_____

_____

_____

2.

I am

adorable

because I am

a delight to behold.

LIST 3 THINGS THAT MAKE YOU ADORABLE.

1. _____

_____

_____

_____

_____

2. _____

_____

_____

_____

_____

3. _____

_____

_____

_____

_____

3.

I am

beautiful

because I can see my own beauty, and I understand that my beauty should never be viewed through society's eyes.

LIST 3 THINGS THAT MAKE YOU BEAUTIFUL.

1. _____

_____

_____

_____

_____

2. _____

_____

_____

_____

_____

3. _____

_____

_____

_____

_____

4.

I am *compassionate* because I understand the importance of being my brothers' and sisters' biggest supporter.

LIST 3 THINGS THAT MAKE YOU COMPASSIONATE.

1. _____

2. _____

3. _____

5.

I am
creative
because I possess
a special ability
to solve problems
in unique ways.

LIST 3 THINGS THAT MAKE YOU CREATIVE.

1. _____

_____

_____

_____

_____

2. _____

_____

_____

_____

_____

3. _____

_____

_____

_____

_____

6.

I am

courageous

because it's in my
DNA to not let fear
stop me from
taking action.

LIST 3 THINGS THAT MAKE YOU COURAGEOUS.

1. _____

_____

_____

_____

_____

2. _____

_____

_____

_____

_____

3. _____

_____

_____

_____

_____

7.

I am

determined

because I understand
that things won't always
come to me easily,
and in order to
achieve my goals, I must
press forward.

GIVE 3 EXAMPLES OF HOW YOU ARE DETERMINED.

1. _____

_____

_____

_____

_____

2. _____

_____

_____

_____

_____

3. _____

_____

_____

_____

_____

8.

I am
diligent
because I understand
that when I work
consistently and
steadily on my goals, my
potential is limitless.

GIVE 3 EXAMPLES OF HOW YOU ARE DILIGENT.

1. _____

_____

_____

_____

_____

2. _____

_____

_____

_____

_____

3. _____

_____

_____

_____

_____

9.

I am

enthusiastic

because I am
interested in and
excited about
the possibilities
for my life.

GIVE 3 EXAMPLES OF HOW YOU ARE ENTHUSIASTIC.

1. ___

___

___

___

___

___

2. ___

___

___

___

___

___

3. ___

___

___

___

___

10.

I am *enough* because God told me so.

GIVE 3 EXAMPLES OF HOW YOU ARE ENOUGH.

1. _____

_____

_____

_____

_____

2. _____

_____

_____

_____

_____

3. _____

_____

_____

_____

_____

II.

I am *frugal* because I understand the power of saving, investing, and building wealth so I can leave a legacy.

GIVE 3 EXAMPLES OF HOW YOU ARE FRUGAL.

1. _____

_____

_____

_____

_____

2. _____

_____

_____

_____

_____

3. _____

_____

_____

_____

_____

12.

I am

fearless

because I am

the descendant

of kings and queens

and it comes

naturally for me.

GIVE 3 EXAMPLES OF YOUR FEARLESSNESS.

1. _____

_____

_____

_____

_____

2. _____

_____

_____

_____

_____

3. _____

_____

_____

_____

_____

13.

I am
friendly
because
I am my sisters'
and brothers'
supporter
and keeper,
and I understand
the power of
relationships.

GIVE 3 EXAMPLES OF HOW YOU ARE FRIENDLY.

1. _____

_____

_____

_____

_____

2. _____

_____

_____

_____

_____

3. _____

_____

_____

_____

_____

14.

I am

fierce

because no
matter how this
world tries to
put me down,
I understand that
I am of exceptional
quality, and I will
keep my head up.

GIVE 3 EXAMPLES OF HOW YOU ARE FIERCE.

1. _____

_____

_____

_____

_____

2. _____

_____

_____

_____

_____

3. _____

_____

_____

_____

_____

15.

I am

funny

because I understand
the importance of
creating joy and
amusement for myself
and others around me.

GIVE 3 EXAMPLES OF HOW YOU ARE FUNNY.

1. _____

_____

_____

_____

_____

2. _____

_____

_____

_____

_____

3. _____

_____

_____

_____

_____

16.

I am

forgiving

because I understand
that holding
a grudge is more
harmful for me than
for the person
who offended me.

GIVE 3 EXAMPLES OF WHEN YOU WERE FORGIVING.

1. _____

2. _____

3. _____

17.

I am *fabulous* because I am capable of extraordinary accomplishments despite obstacles placed in my way.

GIVE 3 EXAMPLES OF HOW YOU ARE FABULOUS.

1. _____

_____

_____

_____

_____

2. _____

_____

_____

_____

_____

3. _____

_____

_____

_____

_____

18.

I am
financially literate
because I understand
that in order to build
wealth and opportunities
for myself and others,
I need to understand the
importance of earning,
saving, investing, and owning
my own business.

LIST 3 THINGS THAT DEMONSTRATE YOU ARE FINANCIALLY LITERATE.

1. _____

_____

_____

_____

_____

2. _____

_____

_____

_____

_____

3. _____

_____

_____

_____

_____

19.

I am

fit

because I understand
that I am at my
best when I consistently
exercise and
when my mind and body
are in great shape.

LIST 3 WAYS IN WHICH YOU ARE FIT.

1. _____

_____

_____

_____

_____

2. _____

_____

_____

_____

_____

3. _____

_____

_____

_____

_____

20.

I am

focused

because I understand

that I get

the most accomplished

when I pay attention to

one goal at a time.

LIST 3 EXAMPLES OF HOW YOU ARE FOCUSED.

1. _____

_____

_____

_____

_____

2. _____

_____

_____

_____

_____

3. _____

_____

_____

_____

_____

21.

I am

generous

because I understand
that there is
no limit to what
I can achieve, and
the more I share with
others, the more
there is for me.

LIST 3 EXAMPLES OF YOUR GENEROSITY.

1. _____

2. _____

3. _____

22.

I am

happy

because I am such

a blessing

to my family,

my friends, and

the world.

LIST 3 THINGS THAT MAKE YOU HAPPY.

1. _____

_____

_____

_____

_____

2. _____

_____

_____

_____

_____

3. _____

_____

_____

_____

_____

23.

I am
healthy
because I understand
that health is wealth,
and my body is a
temple that must
consistently be fed
with healthy foods,
consistent exercise, and
adequate sleep.

LIST 3 EXAMPLES OF HOW YOU ARE HEALTHY.

1. _____

_____

_____

_____

_____

2. _____

_____

_____

_____

_____

3. _____

_____

_____

_____

_____

24.

I am *hard-working* because I understand that working hard and smart will lead to goal achievement.

LIST 3 EXAMPLES OF HOW YOU ARE HARD-WORKING.

1. _____

_____

_____

_____

_____

2. _____

_____

_____

_____

_____

3. _____

_____

_____

_____

_____

25.

I am

honest

because speaking
the truth will set
me free.

LIST 3 EXAMPLES OF WHEN YOU WERE HONEST.

1. _____

2. _____

3. _____

26.

I am
intelligent
because I'm smart
and I can problem-solve
my way out
of any situation.

LIST 3 EXAMPLES THAT SHOW YOUR INTELLIGENCE.

1. _____

_____

_____

_____

_____

2. _____

_____

_____

_____

_____

3. _____

_____

_____

_____

_____

27.

I am *independent* because I am a leader and not a follower, and I won't let other people cause me to make bad decisions.

LIST 3 EXAMPLES THAT SHOW YOUR INDEPENDENCE.

1. _____

_____

_____

_____

_____

2. _____

_____

_____

_____

_____

3. _____

_____

_____

_____

28.

I am *inspirational* because when I do my best, it causes others around me to be their best, and my actions cause a positive change in the world.

LIST 3 EXAMPLES THAT DEMONSTRATE YOU ARE INSPIRATIONAL.

1. _____

_____

_____

_____

_____

2. _____

_____

_____

_____

_____

3. _____

_____

_____

_____

_____

29.

I am
kind
because I am helpful
and considerate
of others.

LIST 3 WAYS IN WHICH YOU ARE KIND.

1. ___

2. ___

3. ___

30.

I am
knowledgeable
because I ensure
that I read
constantly in order
to be well aware
and well informed.

LIST 3 SUBJECTS YOU ARE KNOWLEDGEABLE ABOUT.

1. ___

___

___

___

___

2. ___

___

___

___

___

3. ___

___

___

___

___

31.

I am
love
because I am
deserving of receiving
and giving love
and respect, and I
understand that love
should never hurt or
be abusive.

LIST 3 TIMES WHEN YOU HAVE GIVEN AND RECEIVED LOVE.

1.

2.

3.

32.

I am
loving
because I understand
the power of showing
affection to others.

GIVE 3 EXAMPLES OF WHEN YOU WERE LOVING.

1. _____

_____

_____

_____

_____

2. _____

_____

_____

_____

_____

3. _____

_____

_____

_____

_____

33.

I am *lucky* because I understand that I am responsible for creating my own opportunities and good fortunes.

LIST 3 TIMES WHEN YOU CREATED YOUR OWN LUCK.

1. _____

_____

_____

_____

_____

2. _____

_____

_____

_____

_____

3. _____

_____

_____

_____

_____

34.

....

I am
majestic
because I possess
beauty, dignity, and a
special kind of magic.

GIVE 3 TIMES WHEN YOU FELT MAJESTIC.

1. _____

_____

_____

_____

_____

2. _____

_____

_____

_____

_____

3. _____

_____

_____

_____

_____

35.

I am
magnificent
because I am grand,
I love myself, and
people are in awe of
me and my abilities.

GIVE 3 EXAMPLES OF HOW YOU ARE MAGNIFICENT.

1. _____

_____

_____

_____

_____

2. _____

_____

_____

_____

_____

3. _____

_____

_____

_____

_____

36.

I am

miraculous

because I am here by divine order.

GIVE 3 REASONS WHY YOU ARE MIRACULOUS.

1. _____

2. _____

3. _____

37.

I am

neat

because I don't
operate in chaos.

GIVE 3 EXAMPLES OF HOW YOU ARE NEAT.

1. _____

_____

_____

_____

_____

2. _____

_____

_____

_____

_____

3. _____

_____

_____

_____

_____

38.

I am
optimistic
because I understand that my current situation is never my final destination, and I have the power to turn my life around.

LIST 3 THINGS YOU ARE OPTIMISTIC ABOUT.

1. _____

2. _____

3. _____

39.

I am
open-minded
because I am willing
to try new things,
consider new ideas,
and travel to distant
places.

GIVE 3 EXAMPLES OF HOW YOU ARE OPEN-MINDED.

1. _____

_____

_____

_____

_____

2. _____

_____

_____

_____

_____

3. _____

_____

_____

_____

_____

40.

I am

opulent

because I was made

rich and luxurious,

and I possess

immense potential.

GIVE 3 EXAMPLES OF YOUR OPULENCE.

1. _____

_____

_____

_____

_____

2. _____

_____

_____

_____

_____

3. _____

_____

_____

_____

_____

41.

I am *persistent* because, like Maya Angelo said, no matter what challenges I face, still I rise.

GIVE 3 EXAMPLES OF YOUR PERSISTENCE.

1. _____

_____

_____

_____

_____

2. _____

_____

_____

_____

_____

3. _____

_____

_____

_____

_____

42.

I am
powerful
because I understand
that I have the power
to create the life I
want, and I know
that the solutions are
within me.

LIST 3 TIMES YOU FELT POWERFUL.

1. _____

_____

_____

_____

_____

2. _____

_____

_____

_____

_____

3. _____

_____

_____

_____

_____

43.

I am *quick-witted* because I'm so intelligent, I can quickly cope with new situations.

LIST 3 TIMES YOU FELT QUICK-WITTED.

1. _____

_____

_____

_____

_____

2. _____

_____

_____

_____

_____

3. _____

_____

_____

_____

_____

44.

I am
radiant
because I am a light
to the world, and no
one has permission to
put out my shine.

LIST 3 EXAMPLES OF YOUR RADIANCE.

1. _____

_____

_____

_____

_____

2. _____

_____

_____

_____

_____

3. _____

_____

_____

_____

_____

45.

I am

rich

because I'm equipped
with the knowledge
and the ability to
easily create wealth
for myself and for
those around me.

GIVE 3 WAYS IN WHICH YOU COULD CREATE WEALTH.

1. _____

_____

_____

_____

_____

2. _____

_____

_____

_____

_____

3. _____

_____

_____

_____

_____

46.

I am
reliable
because I can be
trusted to do what
I say I will do.

LIST 3 TIMES YOU WERE RELIABLE.

1. _____

_____

_____

_____

_____

2. _____

_____

_____

_____

_____

3. _____

_____

_____

_____

_____

47.

I am
qualified
because I know how
to level up and
take on any task I set
out to do.

LIST 3 WAYS IN WHICH YOU ARE QUALIFIED.

1. _____

_____

_____

_____

_____

2. _____

_____

_____

_____

_____

3. _____

_____

_____

_____

_____

48.

I am *self-confident* because I believe and trust in my own abilities, even when others don't.

GIVE 3 EXAMPLES TO SHOW YOUR SELF-CONFIDENCE.

1. _____

_____

_____

_____

_____

2. _____

_____

_____

_____

_____

3. _____

_____

_____

_____

_____

49.

I am

sacred

because I am divinely
ordered and was
placed here to do
amazing things.

LIST 3 THINGS THAT MAKE YOU SACRED.

1. _____

2. _____

3. _____

50.

I am

tactical

because I am strategic
in my thinking and
my planning.

LIST EXAMPLES OF WHEN YOU WERE TACTICAL.

1. _____

_____

_____

_____

_____

2. _____

_____

_____

_____

_____

3. _____

_____

_____

_____

_____

51.

I am

smart

because I
understand that
I can do anything
I set my mind to do.

GIVE 3 EXAMPLES OF HOW YOU ARE SMART.

1. _____

_____

_____

_____

_____

2. _____

_____

_____

_____

_____

3. _____

_____

_____

_____

_____

52.

I am
strong
because my ancestors
have withstood
tremendous hardship
just to ensure I am
here, and I can handle
the challenges put
before me.

GIVE 3 EXAMPLES OF WHEN YOU WERE MENTALLY STRONG.

1. _____

_____

_____

_____

_____

2. _____

_____

_____

_____

_____

3. _____

_____

_____

_____

_____

53.

I am *thoughtful* because I understand the importance of being attentive and considerate of others.

LIST 3 THINGS THAT DEMONSTRATE YOUR THOUGHTFULNESS.

1. _____

_____

_____

_____

_____

2. _____

_____

_____

_____

_____

3. _____

_____

_____

_____

_____

54.

I am *unique* because there has never been nor will there ever be another person who possesses my personality, talents, and skills. I am not here by accident.

GIVE 3 EXAMPLES TO SHOW YOUR UNIQUENESS.

1. _____

_____

_____

_____

_____

2. _____

_____

_____

_____

_____

3. _____

_____

_____

_____

_____

55.

I am

versatile

because when I'm
faced with challenges,
I understand those
challenges are there
to provide me with
lessons to help me
quickly adapt.

LIST 3 EXAMPLES OF YOUR VERSATILITY.

1. _____

_____

_____

_____

_____

2. _____

_____

_____

_____

_____

3. _____

_____

_____

_____

_____

56.

I am
valuable
because I know my beauty, strength, and worth, even if others don't know it.

LIST 3 REASONS WHY YOU ARE VALUABLE.

1. _____

_____

_____

_____

_____

2. _____

_____

_____

_____

_____

3. _____

_____

_____

_____

57.

I am *wonderful* because I am wonderfully and beautifully made, and I will never allow someone to abuse me or take advantage of me.

LIST 3 WAYS YOU ARE WONDERFUL.

1. _____

2. _____

3. _____

58.

I am

witty

because I am clever

and funny.

LIST 3 TIMES YOU WERE WITTY.

1. _____

_____

_____

_____

_____

2. _____

_____

_____

_____

_____

3. _____

_____

_____

_____

59.

I am

Zen

because I am in
control of my inner
calm and peace even
in a chaotic world,
and I prioritize
recharging and
replenishing my spirit.

LIST 3 WAYS YOU CAN CREATE ZEN.

1. _____

2. _____

3. _____

60.

I am
zealous
because I am eager and enthusiastic in everything I do.

GIVE 3 EXAMPLES OF YOUR ZEAL.

1. _____

_____

_____

_____

_____

2. _____

_____

_____

_____

_____

3. _____

_____

_____

_____

_____

CREATING DISTINCTIVE BOOKS
WITH INTENTIONAL RESULTS

We're a collaborative group of creative masterminds with a mission to produce high-quality books to position you for monumental success in the marketplace.

Our professional team of writers, editors, designers, and marketing strategists work closely together to ensure that every detail of your book is a clear representation of the message in your writing.

Want to know more?
Write to us at info@publishyourgift.com
or call (888) 949-6228

Discover great books, exclusive offers, and more at
www.PublishYourGift.com

Connect with us on social media

@publishyourgift

www.ingramcontent.com/pod-product-compliance
Lightning Source LLC
LaVergne TN
LVHW022002060526
838200LV00003B/55